Women in Britain

London: H M S O

© Crown copyright 1991
First published 1991

ISBN 0 11 701632 2

 HMSO

HMSO publications are available from:

HMSO Publications Centre
(Mail and telephone orders only)
PO Box 276, London, SW8 5DT
Telephone orders 071-873 9090
General enquiries 071-873 0011
(queuing system in operation for both numbers)

HMSO Bookshops
49 High Holborn, London, WC1V 6HB   071-873 0011 (counter service only)
258 Broad Street, Birmingham, B1 2HE   021-643 3740
Southey House, 33 Wine Street, Bristol, BS1 2BQ   (0272) 264306
9-21 Princess Street, Manchester, M60 8AS   061-834 7201
80 Chichester Street, Belfast, BT1 4JY   (0232) 238451
71 Lothian Road, Edinburgh, EH3 9AZ   031-228 4481

HMSO's Accredited Agents
(see Yellow Pages)
and through good booksellers

Photo Credits

Numbers refer to the pages in the illustration section (1–8): Format Partners
front cover (top left), pp. 6 (bottom left), 7 (top), 8 (bottom); British Gas
front cover (top right and bottom right); *Good Housekeeping* magazine and
Graham Peebles front cover (bottom left); National Portrait Gallery p. 1; Press
Association pp. 2 (top), 3 (top); Hanson PLC p. 2 (bottom); London Features
International p. 3 (bottom); Syndication International p. 4 (top); Universal
Pictorial Press p. 4 (bottom); Allsport p. 5 (top); Rex Features p. 5 (bottom
left); Universal Pictorial Press p. 5 (bottom centre); Camera Press Ltd p. 5
(bottom right); British Airways p. 6 (bottom right).

Contents

Introduction

The role and status of women in Britain[1] have changed substantially in recent decades. Various factors, particularly a growing independence as more women have entered paid employment, have led to higher expectations and a desire for greater participation in all aspects of social and public life. The organisation of family life has altered as a result of social and economic developments, including the decision of increasing numbers of women to combine work and raising a family. Women today play a more active role in areas of public life as diverse as the media, art, sport, business and politics. Important progress towards equality of opportunity has been achieved in the past 20 years through legislation concerning among other things employment, education, training and social welfare. For an historical outline of the development of the social role and status of women, see Appendix II.

Inequalities of opportunity and under-achievement remain in important areas: a disproportionately large number of women workers, for example, are in lower paid, lower status jobs, and they are under-represented in Parliament and in other positions in public and professional life. The under-achievement of many women is seen by the Government as a significant waste of the

---

[1] The term 'Britain' is used informally in this booklet to refer to the United Kingdom of Great Britain and Northern Ireland. 'Great Britain' comprises England, Wales and Scotland.

talent of one-half of the population, which is damaging to Britain's economic prospects.

In responding to these and other problems, the Government's policy is to implement fully and, where necessary, build upon legislation which provides women with a firm basis for pursuing equality of opportunity. It also seeks to initiate and support practical measures aimed at widening opportunities for women in education, training and employment; and, importantly, to create the economic prosperity to provide more job opportunities for both men and women. While encouraging women to follow careers in areas of life traditionally occupied by men, the Government recognises the equally valuable role played by those who choose to work as housewives, mothers and voluntary carers for sick and elderly people.

This booklet describes the contribution made by women to national life; the role played by government departments and agencies concerned with sex equality; legislation relating to the position of women in society; and the progress made towards greater equality in education, employment, social welfare and criminal justice. It also offers a sketch of Britain's contribution to international co-operation in the field of sexual equality. Reference is made to some of the remaining problems of inequality and under-achievement.

The information contained in this booklet is not legally authoritative. For fuller guidance, enquirers should consult the appropriate authorities referred to in the text.

Women in Public Life, Culture, the Media and Sport

Public Life

Women contribute to British public life by serving in government, on public bodies and corporations, in the administration of justice, and in business and the professions, and the trade unions. They also make their views on public issues known through a wide range of women's voluntary organisations and pressure groups. Women enjoy the same political rights as men, and may vote in parliamentary and local elections, be elected to the House of Commons or to local councils and sit in the House of Lords. They can also hold office as government ministers or as mayor, provost (in Scotland) or chairwoman of a local council. Britain has acceded to the 1952 United Nations Convention on the Political Rights of Women.

Politics

Of the 650 members of the House of Commons, 44 are women. In 1979 the then Prime Minister, Mrs Margaret Thatcher, became the first woman in either Western Europe or North America to rise to the highest national political office. Eight women ministers presently serve in the Government. In the House of Lords 61 life peeresses have been appointed in recognition of distinguished service in politics or other fields of public life; there are 313 life peers.

Since 1979 the Labour Party, which currently forms the official Opposition in Parliament, has had a spokesman or woman for women's rights with a post in the shadow cabinet, which must have a minimum of three women members. Both the Labour Party and the Liberal Democrats have a policy of compulsory female representation on constituency shortlists of parliamentary candidates. Mrs Margaret Ewing is parliamentary leader of the Scottish National Party.

The small number of women entering the House of Commons—one of the lowest proportions of any national parliament in Western Europe—has been the subject of considerable comment. Although the number of women parliamentary candidates has increased, women still experience difficulty in being adopted by political parties as candidates for a parliamentary election. Other reasons advanced to explain women's under-representation in Parliament include the long hours and late sittings at the House and the great demands made upon a member's time in dealing with constituency work. These obligations do not combine easily with family life. The Government is at present investigating the possibility of changing House of Commons business hours (normally 14.00 hours to 22.30 hours) to increase the opportunities for women to become MPs.

Women enjoy a proportionately higher representation in the European Parliament: of the 81 British members, 11 are women.

An active role is played by women in the organisations of the political parties at both national and local levels. All of the major parties have a women's organisation. Women are represented on each of the parties' main advisory and decision-making bodies, currently holding 6 seats on the 29-member National Executive Committee of the Labour Party, 53 of the

223 seats on the Conservative Party's National Union Executive Committee, and 10 out of 30 seats on the Liberal Democrats' Federal Policy Committee.

A former journalist, Sarah Hogg, is chief policy adviser to the Prime Minister, Mr John Major.

Public Bodies

It is usual for women to be included in the membership of Royal Commissions and other national and regional advisory committees set up to investigate matters of public concern and to make recommendations to the Government. Some, like Baroness Park, Baroness Platt, Baroness Warnock and Lady Wilcox, have chaired such bodies. Women also serve on administrative bodies such as the boards of nationalised industries and public authorities and on health authorities and tribunals.

Although there has been greater female representation on public bodies over the past few years, the Government is committed to increasing the numbers of women on such bodies. It regards the appointment of more women as beneficial to decision-making and sees women's under-representation as a considerable loss of potential expertise and experience.

In 1990 some 23 per cent of public appointments were held by women compared with 19 per cent in 1986. Much emphasis has been given to women putting their names forward for consideration following the launch in 1986 of the 'Women into Public Life' campaign, organised jointly by the Fawcett Society and the 300 Group (see p. 71), with support from the Government and the Equal Opportunities Commission. The Government's Public Appointments Unit maintains links with women's organisations and seeks to encourage women to serve on public bodies.

Justice

Women play an important role in the administration of justice at the lower levels, comprising some 12,600 out of a total of about 28,700 magistrates in England and Wales. However, they remain poorly represented in the ranks of the judiciary: there is one woman Lord Justice out of a total of 27, two High Court judges out of 83, 20 circuit judges out of 428, 8 stipendiary magistrates out of 64 and 7 county court registrars out of 222. In 1987 Dame Elizabeth Butler-Sloss became the first woman judge to be appointed to the Court of Appeal. In Scotland, in 1990 there were 24 male senators of the College of Justice and no women senators; 6 Sheriffs Principal, all male, and 91 male sheriffs and 4 female sheriffs.

Business and the Professions

Industry and commerce have traditionally been male-dominated areas but greater numbers of women are beginning to rise to the most senior positions. Large corporations like British Petroleum, Grand Metropolitan, Schweppes, Thorn EMI, Woolworth's and GEC have appointed women either to their boards of directors or to take charge of subsidiary firms. In 1990 Caledonian Airways was the first airline in Britain to appoint a female managing director.

Nevertheless, there is still a relative scarcity of women in top management positions and in certain industries and professions. Although women make up over 40 per cent of the British workforce, only 4 per cent of middle and senior managers are women. Women are seriously under-represented in many professions: for example, only 1 per cent of engineers, 3 per cent of surgeons, 6 per cent of surveyors, 8 per cent of architects and 10 per cent of chartered accountants are women. (See *Women in the Professions*, Further Reading.) There are very large numbers of women in the teaching profession: four-fifths of teachers in primary and nearly one-half in secondary schools are female. However, fewer than half of primary school head teachers and only one-sixth of secondary school head teachers are women. While nearly half of civil servants are women, only 10 per cent of senior posts are occupied by women (see pp. 38–41). At the BBC, over two-fifths of the workforce is female, but only a tenth of senior managers and less than one-fifth of middle managers are women.

Trade Unions

Women are active in the trade union movement, making up about a third of the total membership. They predominate in certain trade unions, such as the Union of Shop, Distributive and Allied Workers. In many unions a disproportionately low number of women is to be found among executive council members, full-time officials and delegates to the Trades Union Congress (TUC). Several unions have sought to correct this by positive action, including the operation of quotas for the number of women serving on their decision-making committees. There are at present four women leaders of trade unions: Diana Warwick of the Association of University Teachers; Elizabeth Symons of the Civil Service union the First Division Association; Catherine Burns of the Health

Visitors' Association; and Helen McGrath of the National Union of Hosiery and Knitwear Workers.

Some 17 of the 55 seats on the TUC General Council—the national centre of the trade union movement in Britain—are held by women, and a woman has been president of the TUC on several occasions. A women's advisory committee advises the TUC on issues relating to women workers, and a TUC women's conference sets the agenda for the work of the committee.

Culture

The contribution of women to British cultural life has broadened in recent years as they have entered areas of artistic activity, such as theatre direction and orchestral conducting, previously occupied mainly by men.

Leading authors include Iris Murdoch, Muriel Spark, P.D. James (who is a member of the BBC Board of Governors, the British Council and other national cultural bodies), Penelope Lively, Margaret Drabble, A.S. Byatt and Anita Brookner. In order to widen the availability of works by less well-known women authors, some of whom write from a feminist viewpoint, a few publishing houses have been established which deal exclusively with their work. The Virago Press, for example, publishes some 80 titles each year by both past and present women writers. It has revived many British and foreign classics and accepts for publication manuscripts which it considers have long lacked due recognition.

British actresses have played a distinguished role in the theatre, television and cinema. Among actresses who enjoy international reputations are Dame Wendy Hiller, Vanessa Redgrave, Dame Judi Dench and Glenda Jackson. It is felt by many that insufficient scope is given to the talents of women as playwrights, directors and producers and this has led to the establishment of several all-women theatre companies, including the Women's Theatre Group. Deborah Warner is one of Britain's leading theatre directors, and of women stage designers Alison Chitty is one of the best known.

Comedy has tended to be a male-dominated area, but in recent years several women comedians have enjoyed success in television and films; these include Julie Walters, Victoria Wood and Tracey Ullman, and Dora Bryan on stage.

In the field of classical music, composers such as Thea Musgrave and the late Elisabeth Lutyens have achieved distinguished reputations. Musicians such as Evelyn Glennie, the percussionist; Jane Glover, musical director of the Glyndebourne Touring Opera since 1984; and Iona Brown, director of the Academy of St Martin-in-the-Fields since 1974, have been successful in an area of music where men have previously predominated.

Women performers proliferate in pop and rock music and to a lesser extent in jazz. Kate Bush, Alison Moyet, Annie Lennox and Joan Armatrading have all enjoyed success in the pop and rock field, while Barbara Thompson and Annie Whitehead have established strong reputations as jazz musicians.

In the visual arts, two sculptors, Dame Elisabeth Frink and the late Dame Barbara Hepworth, are among Britain's best-known artists. Seven of the 50 Academicians of the Royal Academy (one of the highest distinctions awarded to artists) are women.

Media

Women play an increasingly important role in the mass media. Jane Drabble is the BBC's assistant managing director, network television; Liz Forgan is director of programmes at Channel 4 (Britain's second independent television service); Janet Street-Porter is the BBC's head of youth programmes; and Jenny Abramsky is BBC Radio 4's editor of news and current affairs. Female programme presenters and newsreaders on both television and radio, such as Sue Lawley, Selina Scott, Joan Bakewell and Sue MacGregor, have become household names. Leading female radio and television reporters include Elinor Goodman, Jane Peel, Sue Cameron, Kate Adie and Carol Barnes. The upper layers of management in the television and radio industries remain male-dominated. Over a fifth of employees on newspapers and magazines are women, the greatest numbers working in magazine journalism. Women are found in reasonable numbers as columnists, departmental heads and editors, especially on magazines. However, there is still a strong tendency for higher positions to be occupied by men.

The most celebrated women newspaper journalists include Eve Pollard, Mary Goldring, Mary Holland, Mary Kenny, Barbara Amiel and Julie Welch (a sports reporter). Posy Simmonds is Britain's best-known woman cartoonist.

Sport

Women engage in most sports and games played in Britain, and the numbers participating have risen considerably in recent years as part of the general growth in active recreation. Men still outnumber women: an estimated 4·9 million women play indoor sport and 5·7 million outdoor sport, compared with 7·4 and 8·6 million men respectively. Moreover, participation among certain groups of women, such as housewives with young children, and women from ethnic minority groups, is well below the national average. Additionally, women are poorly represented in sports-coaching, administration and management, and in sports media. A major priority in official development plans for sport is to narrow the gap between men and women in active sport and recreation.

A more positive attitude towards physical fitness has led to growing participation by women in athletic events like the triple jump and marathon. Women also take part more in 'physical-contact' sports such as association and rugby football, which were previously regarded as 'unfeminine'. Sports from which they had previously been excluded by tradition, rather than on the grounds of physical differences, are similarly increasing in popularity among women: for instance, larger numbers now play snooker and darts.

Many sports have separate governing bodies for women and competitive events are normally organised in separate divisions for men and women. One notable exception is equestrianism, where women riders compete on equal terms with men. Mixed events in which teams of men and women play together are traditional in sports such as tennis, badminton, and ice-skating, and have been growing in popularity in golf.

Lacrosse and netball are played predominantly by women; these, together with tennis, badminton, athletics, hockey, swimming and gymnastics, are the sports most usually played by girls at school.

Pressure from schools is leading to the inclusion of girls in formerly all-boy sports teams, particularly soccer teams at junior level. Men's and women's governing bodies are amalgamating increasingly, and women are encouraged to adopt leadership positions in coaching and administration.

The single-sex arrangements operated in sport are regarded by some as discriminatory; they believe that women should be permitted to compete with men on equal terms in the same events. This, however, would involve amendments to the Sex Discrimination Act 1975, which exempts most competitive sport from its scope. As this is thought to be a minority view, such legislative action does not enjoy the support of the Sports Councils or of the governing bodies of sport. Nonetheless, the Sports Councils are working to remove unnecessary discrimination on the part of sporting bodies.

Government Responsibilities

Overall responsibility for policy on sex equality in Britain is exercised by the Home Office. Individual government departments formulate policies in their specific areas, for example, the Department of Employment is concerned with equal pay and other employment matters. The Equal Opportunities Commission and the Equal Opportunities Commission for Northern Ireland are responsible for the day-to-day administration of sex-equality legislation, the promotion of equal opportunities and other practical matters (see p. 14).

Ministerial Group on Women's Issues

The main forum for co-ordinating the work of government departments and for developing inter-departmental initiatives is the Ministerial Group on Women's Issues under the chairmanship of the Home Office Minister responsible for equal opportunities, at present Mrs Angela Rumbold. Formed in 1986, the Group's membership comprises those ministers with responsibilities for issues of special interest to women, such as health, employment and education.

The Ministerial Group gives government ministers the opportunity to examine and discuss women's issues and to co-ordinate the Government's response in priority areas like childcare, public appointments, domestic violence and the special needs of women from ethnic minorities. Model instructions prepared by the Group are the basis for anti-discrimination guidelines by government departments to their officials so that the impact of policy proposals upon women is fully understood. All legislative proposals are considered against a guidance checklist drawn up by the Group to ensure that they do not give rise to discrimination. This is being reinforced by seminars for senior civil servants. A new informal women's advisory network was formed by Mrs Rumbold in October 1991 to discuss women's issues with ministers.

One of the first tasks of the Ministerial Group was to review British government policy in areas covered by *The Nairobi Forward-Looking Strategies for the Advancement of Women to the Year 2000* agreed at an international conference in 1985; a report was published in 1987 (see p. 72). In January 1990 the Group presented the British Government's initial report on the implementation of the United Nations Convention on the Elimination of All Forms of Discrimination Against Women (CEDAW) to the CEDAW committee in New York (see p. 73).

Equal Opportunities Commission

The Equal Opportunities Commission, set up by the Government in 1975, has powers to enforce the Sex Discrimination Acts and the Equal Pay Act in Great Britain. Northern Ireland has its own sex discrimination laws and a separate commission with similar powers and duties. The Commission consists of a full-time chairman or woman and 12 part-time members. In 1990–91 it received a government grant of £4·6 million.

The statutory duties of the Equal Opportunities Commission are to work towards eliminating discrimination and to promote equality of opportunity. It advises people of their rights under the law and may give financial or other assistance to help individuals to conduct a case before a court or tribunal. In most cases, complaints of discrimination are dealt with by industrial tribunals since they concern employment; others may be taken before county courts in England and Wales and the Sheriff Court in Scotland.

The Commission also has powers to conduct investigations and to issue notices requiring discriminatory practices to stop. In addition, it keeps legislation under review and may submit proposals for amending it to government ministers. The Commission undertakes research, educational and publicity work.

The Sex Discrimination Act 1975 makes it unlawful to discriminate in employment, training and related matters in Great Britain on the grounds of sex, or against married people. Discriminatory advertisements which breach the Act are also unlawful. The employment provisions were amended by the Sex Discrimination Act 1986 to bring British legislation into line with a European Community directive on equal treatment. In addition, the Employment Act 1989 contains provisions to promote equality of opportunity in employment and vocational training, and to meet European Community obligations by repealing most legislation that discriminated in employment between women and men. In Great Britain the Equal Pay Act 1970, as amended in 1984, requires that a woman doing the same, or broadly similar, work as a man, or work which has an equal value, should receive equal pay and conditions of employment.

Practical advice to employers and others on the best arrangements for implementing equal opportunities policies is given in the Commission's codes of practice relating to sexual harassment, elimination of sex and marriage discrimination at work and other matters.

There is similar legislation on sex discrimination and equal pay in Northern Ireland.

A fuller outline of the sex discrimination and equal opportunities laws is given on pp. 17–26. The Equal Opportunities Commission's strategy for promoting equal opportunities in the 1990s is described in Appendix I. A similar strategy is followed by the Equal Opportunities Commission for Northern Ireland.

Women's National Commission

Some 50 of the main national women's organisations are represented on the Women's National Commission, an official advisory committee with a government co-chairman appointed by the Prime Minister. Its purpose is to ensure that the informed opinions of women are given due weight in the deliberations of government. The government co-chairman or woman represents the Commission on the Ministerial Group on Women's Issues.

Recent reports produced by the Commission have covered homelessness, women in prison, lone-parent families and debt. Every two or three years the Commission holds a major conference on a topic of particular interest to women; the 1990 conference took carers as its theme. The Commission co-ordinates responses from women's organisations to a large range of consultative documents.

The Legal Framework

In most respects women have the same legal rights as men. They may acquire, own, use and dispose of property, enter into contracts, and sue and be sued. Women are called to give evidence in legal proceedings, serve on juries under the same conditions as men and subject to the same qualifications, and they are employed as magistrates and judges.

These rights and duties apply to married as well as to single women. A married woman may not only enter into a contract with a third person independently of her husband, and claim damages independently for a civil wrong, but may also make a legally binding contract with her husband and sue him for breach of contract or other civil wrong. The rights of husbands and wives in respect of property and children are practically equal, and women are entitled to equal treatment in divorce settlements.

The criminal law in general applies equally to men and women, providing the same range of penalties for the same offence, and the same protection to the accused.

These legal rights have been acquired by women over the years, and since 1970 Parliament has enacted major legislation to promote equality of opportunity and to eliminate discrimination in many other fields, including employment and education. Among the most recent advances has been the achievement of greater equality in taxation and family law and in entitlement to social security benefits.

Most of the following legislation applies to Great Britain, but Northern Ireland has parallel laws (see p. 26).

Equal Pay Act 1970

The purpose of the Equal Pay Act 1970 is to eliminate discrimination between men and women in Great Britain with regard to pay and other terms of their contracts of employment, for example, overtime, bonuses, output and piecework payments, and holiday and sick-leave entitlement. The Act came into force in 1975.

The Equal Pay Act established the right to equal pay if a woman is employed on work which is the same as, or broadly similar to, that of a man; or on a job which, although different from that of a man, has been given an equal value under a job evaluation scheme. The Act was widened in 1984 to allow a woman to claim equal pay for work of equal value where no job evaluation study has been conducted. In 1984 in the first successful case to be heard under the new regulations, a canteen cook won the right to equal pay with painters, joiners and heating engineers working at the same shipyard.

If a woman considers that she is entitled to equal pay, she can raise the matter with her employer or trade union. When agreement cannot be reached with the employer, she can seek help from the independent Advisory, Conciliation and Arbitration Service, and ultimately go to an industrial tribunal for a decision. Industrial tribunals may refer a case to an independent expert who will prepare a report on the relative value of the two jobs under comparison.

There have been developments in the case law relating to the Equal Pay Act which are beneficial to women. These include:

—removal of the six-month limit on claims under the Act;

—establishing the importance of analytical job evaluation in equal value cases;

—the right for a woman claiming equal pay to have each individual term of contract considered and uprated to that of a comparable male even if her overall remuneration package is greater than his; and

—the right of a woman to compare herself with a man or men doing work of possibly equal value even if there is a man or men doing the same work as the woman for the same pay.

Sex Discrimination Act 1975

The Sex Discrimination Act makes discrimination between men and women on the grounds of sex unlawful in employment and training; education; the provision of housing, goods, facilities and services; and in related advertising. It defines two types of discrimination:

—direct discrimination, which arises when a person is treated less favourably than another on the grounds of his or her sex;

—indirect discrimination, which involves the application of conditions which, though equal in a formal sense, in practice favour one sex or the other.

For a claim of direct discrimination to be valid, the circumstances of the man and woman must be similar.

Employment and Training

It is unlawful for an employer to discriminate in arrangements made for the recruiting and engaging of new employees, and in the treatment of existing employees in matters such as promotion, training, transfer and dismissal. Training may be given under the Act on a single-sex basis for work in which comparatively few members of one sex were engaged over the previous 12 months, to encourage individuals of that sex to take advantage of opportunities for doing such work, and for people who have not been working because of domestic or family responsibilities (see pp. 41–44).

Education

Local education authorities and school governing bodies, which provide the state education system, have a general duty to ensure that their facilities are available without sex discrimination. It is unlawful for a co-educational school, college or university to discriminate regarding attendance; a college cannot, for example, decide to admit a certain quota of men or women irrespective of their qualifications. This stipulation does not apply to single-sex schools or colleges. Once admitted to a co-educational establishment, pupils must have equal access to the curriculum and equal opportunities to use the facilities available. A girl cannot, for instance, be refused entry to a woodwork class on the grounds of sex, and similarly a boy cannot be refused entry to a home economics course. The Act does not prohibit the provision of separate facilities for boys and girls where these are considered appropriate, for example, in physical education. Also, it is permissible to offer single-sex classes in subjects where research shows that single-sex groups attain better results.

Other aspects of education covered by the Act include the award of grants to students, and the advice and assistance given to school-leavers by careers and other local education authority services.

Housing, Goods, Facilities and Services

It is unlawful under the Act, with certain exceptions, to discriminate against a man or woman when selling or letting land, houses, flats and business premises. People providing goods, facilities and services must not discriminate against a woman either by refusing them or by supplying them on less favourable terms than to a man.

Advertising

It is unlawful to publish, or place for publication, advertisements which are discriminatory, or which indicate an intention to discriminate. A job advertisement using a description such as 'waiter', 'salesman' or 'steward' must point out that both men and women are eligible.

Enforcement

The procedures for dealing with complaints alleging sex discrimination differ according to the subject of the complaint. Employment complaints are dealt with by industrial tribunals, and most other complaints by courts of law. Complaints about the education system must first be considered by the appropriate education minister before court action can be taken.

Sex Discrimination Act 1986

The Sex Discrimination Act 1986 was designed to bring British law into line with the European Community directive on equal treatment and to remove sex discrimination in British employment legislation.

Under the Sex Discrimination Act 1975, private households and businesses with five or fewer employees were exempted from a requirement of the Act not to discriminate between the sexes in employment practices. The 1986 Act provided for a more limited exemption for private households, while maintaining the principle of respect for private life; the exemption enjoyed by firms employing five or fewer people was removed. The 1986 Act also outlawed discriminatory elements in collective agreements, internal rules of undertakings, and rules governing independent occupations and professions. It lifted legal restrictions on women's hours of work which prevented them from working shifts and at night, stipulated the maximum number of hours that they could work, and curtailed overtime working. In the light of this change, restrictions on night baking by men were abolished to ensure that there would be no discrimination against men.

The 1986 Act also gave men and women doing similar work the right to retire at the same age. A judgment of the European Court of Justice stated in 1986 that it was an act of sex discrimination for an employer to dismiss a woman solely because she had reached the qualifying age for a state pension, which in Britain is different from the qualifying age for men. Under the 1986 Act, women have the right to continue working until the same age as men in those occupations that have different retirement ages for men and women. This change did not, however, affect rights of access to occupational or state pensions (see pp. 59–60).

Rights of Expectant Mothers

The Employment Protection Act 1975 gave important rights to a working woman expecting a baby. Women with two years' service working for more than 16 hours a week, and women with five years' service employed for between eight and 16 hours a week, have the right not to be unfairly dismissed because of pregnancy, except in limited circumstances. They are also entitled to return to work not later than 29 weeks after the birth of the baby.

Under the Employment Act 1980, women employees who are pregnant cannot be unreasonably refused time off for ante-natal care and must be paid for the time off. These rights exist irrespective of length of service or hours worked.

Details of the statutory maternity pay scheme and other maternity benefits are given on pp. 55–6.

Similar provisions are in force in Northern Ireland.

Social Security

The Social Security Pensions Act 1975 introduced the State Earnings Related Pension Scheme under which women earners receive the same benefits as men. It also laid down that women should have equal access to occupational pension schemes. Unequal treatment persists, however, in certain occupational schemes in terms of access to, and levels of benefit for, part-time workers.

The Act protects the entitlement to basic pension for people unable to work because of domestic responsibilities, such as care of elderly and invalid relatives, as well as childcare.

The Social Security Act 1980 provides for equality of entitlement to personal social security benefits, allowances for dependent children, and short-term National Insurance benefits for dependent adults. Women thus have the same right as men to claim unemployment and sickness benefit for their spouses and children.

Immigration and Nationality

The rights of women under immigration and nationality laws were extended by the British Nationality Act 1981, and are now substantially the same as those enjoyed by men. Under the Act, women have gained the right to transmit British citizenship, on equal terms with men, to their children born overseas. Also, British women have, subject to certain tests, acquired the right to bring into the country a foreign husband or fiancé.

Matrimonial and Family Law

A number of reforms to matrimonial and family law affecting women have been implemented in recent years. In England and Wales, the Matrimonial and Family Proceedings Act 1984 relaxed the time restrictions on the presentation of divorce petitions and reformed the legal framework for making financial settlements on divorce. These changes were designed to give the courts further scope to deal with the problems which arise on marital breakdown. The relevant law applies equally to both spouses. One of the primary objects of the Family Law Reform Act 1987 was to remove legal discrimination against children born outside marriage. The Act also had the effect of making it easier to obtain maintenance for such children from absent parents. The Children Act 1989 makes important reforms to child law generally, including the law relating to custody and guardianship, and emphasises the responsibility of both parents for their children.

In Scotland the Law Reform (Husband and Wife) (Scotland) Act 1984 abolished rules that were obsolete and discriminatory. The Family Law (Scotland) Act 1985 was designed to promote greater fairness and consistency in financial provision on divorce, and clarified the law on the property rights and legal capacity of married couples. The Law Reform (Parent and Child) (Scotland) Act 1986 removed or amended provisions which discriminated against illegitimate children and their parents.

Personal Taxation

A new system of independent taxation for husband and wife was introduced in April 1990 under the Finance Act 1988. Before that date the income of a married woman was generally treated as if it belonged to her husband. The new system gives married women greatly increased privacy and independence in tax affairs and ends certain tax penalties on marriage.

All taxpayers, irrespective of marital status, are responsible for paying tax on their own income and are entitled to a personal allowance to be set against any income they may have. The tax system continues to recognise marriage through the provision of a married couple's allowance which, in practice, may be claimed by either the husband or wife. Similarly, husbands and wives are now taxed independently on any capital gains. Independent taxation eliminates the most common tax penalty, the taxation of a married woman's income (including investment income) at her husband's higher rate.

Other Employment Measures

The Employment Act 1989 replaced or amended most legislation that discriminated between men and women in employment and training, and in so doing meets European Community obligations. The ban on women working underground in mines and quarries was removed, as were some restrictions on their working with machinery in factories. Nevertheless, protection is retained in special cases such as work which, through exposure to radiation or lead, might endanger the health of an unborn child. Also, under the Act, women become eligible to receive statutory redundancy payments up to the same age—65—as men.

Northern Ireland

Sex discrimination legislation in Northern Ireland parallels that in the rest of Britain. The Sex Discrimination (Northern Ireland) Order 1976, and the Equal Pay Act (Northern Ireland) 1970, broadly replicate equivalent provision in Great Britain. The Employment Act 1989 was extended to Northern Ireland by the Employment (Miscellaneous Provisions) (Northern Ireland) Order 1990.

Education

The development of equal opportunities has a special importance in education for widening women's career prospects and
influencing attitudes towards women's place in society. The
Government is committed to promoting equal opportunities in
schools, colleges and universities and to encouraging girls and
young women to study traditionally male-dominated disciplines
such as science and engineering.

Significant advances have been made in recent years:
legal and structural barriers to educational equality have been
removed by the Sex Discrimination Act 1975 and other
measures, and there has been a sharp rise in the number of
girls and young women entering further and higher education.
The main remaining difficulty is the continuing tendency of
girls and young women at all levels of education to concentrate
on studying arts and other subjects traditionally regarded as
'feminine'. It is now widely recognised that the growing
importance to the economy of advances in science and technology will require many more women to acquire scientific and
technological skills. The priority given in further and higher
education to scientific and technological courses has, moreover,
reduced the number of arts courses available, and with them
the most common route for young women to higher education
and the professions.

The Government believes that the problem does not
require further legislation, but rather a change in the attitude

of parents, teachers, school governors and of girls and women themselves, and in the provision of more single-sex courses where this is appropriate.

Schools

Full-time attendance at school is obligatory for both girls and boys between the ages of five (four in Northern Ireland) and 16. However, many children under five attend nursery schools and classes and infants' classes in primary schools. The proportion of children aged three or four attending such classes has risen from around one-sixth in 1966 to around a half of all children in that age range. Boys and girls are taught together in most primary schools. More than 80 per cent of pupils in maintained secondary schools in England and Wales, and nearly all schools in Scotland, are mixed. There is also a growing trend in the independent sector, including most of the well-known public schools which formerly admitted only boys, towards the provision of mixed education.

The Government does not want girls to limit their career prospects by dropping the study of science, technology and certain other subjects too early in their school education. The Education Reform Act 1988 states that the school curriculum should prepare young people for the experiences, opportunities and responsibilities of adult life. With the introduction in 1989 of the National Curriculum, girls in England and Wales follow the same broad and balanced curriculum as boys up to the age of 16, thereby removing any discrimination and stereotyping in subject choice. Cross-curricular themes are designed to help focus attention on sex discrimination and stereotyping, encouraging positive changes in attitude. Schools must ensure that their programmes of work-related activities are free of stereotyping and that they pay particular attention to equal opportunities. Parallel reforms have been carried out in Scotland and Northern Ireland.

Some local education authorities and schools have appointed advisers, and others have designated teacher-advisers to work on equal opportunities measures.

Special Initiatives

Three major initiatives aimed at preparing schoolchildren for working life have emphasised the need to avoid sex-stereotyping in courses and teaching materials. Equality of opportunity is an integral part of the Technical and Vocational Education Initiative which is designed to make the curriculum of 14- to 18-year-olds more relevant to adult and working life. Government-financed schemes supporting the use of micro-computers in schools have also given special emphasis to the development of courses and teaching materials which avoid stereotyping. City Technology Colleges, providing broad-based education with a strong technological and business element, are required to adopt equal opportunities policies as a condition of funding. Pupils are selected in accordance with objective criteria irrespective of sex.

As a result of these and other initiatives, it is expected that more girls will take up science, engineering and technological subjects and subsequently follow scientific and technological careers.

Examination Results

Examination results show a progressive reduction in sex-stereotyping in schools as well as a steady improvement in the performance of girls in examinations. Over the last ten years there has been a growth in the proportion of girls taking chemistry at General Certificate of Education (GCE) or General Certificate of Secondary Education (GCSE) level: about one in four in 1988, compared with one in six in 1979. In 1988 one in five girls took physics compared with one in eight in 1979. Overall, girls achieved greater examination success than boys in 1988 in the GCSE and equivalent levels. Proportionately, boys were more successful than girls in attaining three or more GCE Advanced levels.

In Scotland, latest statistics show that more girls than boys leave school with qualifications.

Further and Higher Education

One of the Government's priorities for student recruitment in further and higher education[1] is to provide more opportunities for women, particularly for mature students with domestic responsibilities. Measures designed to encourage female recruitment include improving guidance and information about opportunities and promoting more flexible forms of provision such as open learning schemes.

---

[1] Under the Education Reform Act 1988, higher education comprises courses of a standard higher than GCE Advanced level or its equivalent, and further education all other post-school courses.

Between 1980 and 1988 the total of full-time women higher education students rose substantially, the numbers of undergraduates rising by 74 per cent and postgraduates by 78 per cent (compared with rises of 91 per cent and 89 per cent, respectively, for men). Women formed over 43 per cent of higher education enrolments in 1988–89, compared with 40 per cent in 1979. In 1988 women comprised 48 per cent of all first year full-time mature higher education students and 42 per cent of first year part-time mature higher education students; in 1979 the respective figures were 41 and 27 per cent.

As in schools, women are strongly represented on arts and other courses such as education, but less strongly in science and technology, making up, for example, over 70 per cent of undergraduates in languages and literature but under 11 per cent in engineering and technology. There have, however, been increases in the numbers of women taking degrees in science subjects, social administration, business studies and certain technical subjects. To encourage more women to study science and technology subjects, some universities, polytechnics and colleges of further and higher education, run short introductory 'conversion' courses at the beginning of a science or technology degree course. These enable applicants with arts qualifications or late starters to attain the required standard.

Women form the majority in further education and outnumber men by three to one on adult education courses, due in part to the flexibility and accessibility of the courses, many being part-time or taught at evening classes.

One-year 'access' courses, run by further and higher education establishments, enable older women (and men) with non-standard entry qualifications to gain entry to higher education. The courses are designed to meet the needs of identified groups, including women, which are under-represented in higher education. Some access courses cater exclusively for women in, for instance, micro-electronics, engineering, information technology and industrial technology. The growth of access courses has been very rapid in recent years; there are now about 600 courses on offer in Britain.

The Open University

A development which brought higher education within the range of large numbers of women was the establishment in 1969 of the Open University. Just under half of students on undergraduate and other courses in 1990 were women. The University is particularly suited to women's needs with its flexible study hours and course arrangements, enabling students to organise study around their normal working and domestic circumstances.

The University is non-residential, offering degree and other courses for adult students of all ages throughout Britain. In 1991 there were 75,000 registered undergraduates, and in all 108,000 first degrees have been awarded since the University's inception. In the main it uses a combination of specially produced printed texts, correspondence tuition, television and radio broadcasts, audio and video cassettes, and residential schools, together with a network of study centres for contact with part-time tutors and counsellors, and with fellow students.

No formal academic qualifications are required to register for courses, but the standards of the University's degrees are the same as at other universities. Its first degree is the BA (Open), a general degree awarded on a system of credits for each course completed. The University also has a programme of higher degrees, available through research and taught courses.

Programmes of study are also available for professionals in education and the health and social services, and for up-dating managers, scientists and technologists.

Employment

More women are employed or seeking employment in Britain today than ever before. Later marriages and effective methods of family planning have led to a decline in family size, with the result that women tend to be absent from the labour force for domestic reasons for a relatively short time. The number of women who have younger children and who return to work has increased rapidly. Other reasons for the growth of the female workforce are: the higher divorce rate and the rise in births outside marriage, leading to larger numbers of lone-parent families (one in six of all families with children), more than nine-tenths of which are headed by women; the need to supplement the husband's income; and the desire of many women to fulfil themselves through work. The changing character of the British economy, with the expansion of service sector industries such as banking and insurance, and the growth in part-time employment, has given women wider working opportunities.

Women comprise more than two-fifths of the British workforce (some 12 million out of a total of 28 million), a higher proportion than in any other European Community country except Denmark. Since the second world war (1939–45) the proportion of working married women has grown to two-thirds of those between the ages of 16 and 59, and they now make up over one-quarter of the labour force compared with only 4 per cent in 1921. As many women combine work

and raising a family, and because their earnings have traditionally supplemented those of their husbands, 43 per cent of all
women in employment work part-time, representing 87 per
cent of all part-time workers.

Women have traditionally been concentrated in certain
types of job and industries, and over three-quarters now work
in the service sector. About a fifth of female manual workers in
Great Britain (two-thirds in Northern Ireland) are employed in
catering, cleaning, hairdressing and other personal services and
occupations, and many more are in semi-skilled factory jobs and
retailing. Of non-manual working women, a little under half
work in clerical and related office jobs and two-fifths in professional and related occupations in education, welfare and health.

In certain sectors women have always been well represented. Around four-fifths of state primary school teachers and
nearly half of secondary school teachers are women. The
National Health Service (NHS) employs more women than any
other organisation in Britain: out of a total workforce of
1,150,000, 910,000 are women. Three-quarters are qualified
staff—doctors, nurses, physiotherapists and technical staff.

Women working full-time in non-manual jobs often enjoy
markedly better conditions and opportunities than the majority
of working women. They are better paid and generally have
superior fringe benefits and opportunities for training and
promotion. They are also more likely to belong to trade unions,
and unionised employment tends to command better pay and
conditions.

The majority of women who change jobs do so for work-
related, rather than for domestic, reasons. However, if women
do leave the labour force and re-enter it after childbearing, a

substantial minority return at a lower level than that at which they left; this is particularly so if they return to the labour market only part-time, and is more likely the longer the return is delayed.

The Government is fully committed to the principle and practice of equality for men and women at work and actively encourages employers to adopt equal opportunities practices. Although women's average hourly earnings were only 77 per cent of men's in 1990, the last three years have shown a progressive rise in women's hourly rates.

The Advisory Committee on Women's Employment advises the Government on questions of employment policy relating to women. Members include the chairwoman of the Equal Opportunities Commission, representatives from politics, industry and trade unions, and several independent members appointed because of their experience of women's education, training or employment.

Developments

The Government has sought to create an economic climate in which business can flourish and hence provide more jobs for both men and women. Since 1984 over 1·2 million women have entered the labour force; 15 per cent more are working in full-time employment and 13 per cent more part-time. The number of self-employed women has more than doubled since 1979 and women now account for one in four of the self-employed in Great Britain and one in six in Northern Ireland; nearly a third of entrants to the Enterprise Allowance Scheme[1] are women.

[1] A government scheme for helping unemployed people wishing to start their own businesses.

Women are gaining more educational and vocational qualifications and entering areas of employment traditionally dominated by men. Half of the students in medicine, dentistry and other health services are women. Since 1980 the number of women accountants has doubled; that of women surveyors quadrupled; town planners doubled; and in banking and insurance numbers have increased by one-third. Female unemployment, at 5 per cent, remains lower than male unemployment, which is around 11 per cent.

An indication of women's progress in breaking down traditional barriers has been the achievements of women in the armed forces: in 1982, for example, a woman took command of a British Army unit for the first time and in the same year the first woman Commander of a Royal Air Force operational station was appointed, with responsibility for the air defence of one-third of Britain. In the army, women are employed in peace and war in all posts except where the primary role is direct combat. The Royal Navy now allows women to serve at sea.

The only vocations to which women are not admitted are the ministries of the Anglican and Roman Catholic Churches, although in 1984 the governing body of the Church of England voted in favour of legislation to permit the ordination of women.

Changes in the labour market, particularly a projected fall of one million in the number of 16- to 19-year-olds entering the job market between 1984 and 1994, are expected to bring further opportunities for women. It is thought that up to the year 2001 women will account for more than 95 per cent of the total increase in the size of the workforce.

Employers are becoming increasingly aware of the need to tailor recruitment, training and general employment policies so that they are fair and attractive to women. Major employers, such as Esso, BP, ICI, IBM, leading banks and the Civil Service have introduced schemes to allow women to interrupt their careers to bring up children. Other measures being considered, or already introduced, include job-sharing schemes, school term-time only contracts, part-time working and assistance with childcare. Opportunity 2000 is a private-sector initiative which aims to set female recruitment and promotion targets for the year 2000.

In October 1990 local authorities launched a campaign to improve the working environment for women employees in order to ease recruitment and retention problems. Also, a register of retired local government workers available for consultancy work is being compiled. An outline of public and private sector initiatives on childcare provision is provided on pp. 61–64.

Government as Employer

The Government has had a formal programme of action to achieve equality of opportunity for women staff since 1984. The programme provides for working practices which enable staff to combine a career with other responsibilities, thereby helping to improve staff stability, development and retention. It also stresses the need to ensure that women enjoy equality of access to jobs at every level. As a major employer, the Government sets an example by:

—increasing opportunities for flexible working patterns (including term-time and home-working) and for part-time working and job sharing at senior as well as junior levels;

—providing financial assistance for childcare facilities (see p. 61);

—granting enhanced maternity leave;

—providing paternity leave.

Already well over 200 senior civil servants work part-time, and in total 6 per cent of all staff, the majority women, work part-time or job share, compared with only four per cent in 1986. Some 12 per cent of female staff are part-timers or job sharers. Generally, part-time staff are employed on the same terms and conditions as full-time staff. All major government departments operate keeping-in-touch arrangements for staff who resign for domestic reasons, in order to encourage reinstatement and to enable staff to maintain their familiarity with work and their skill-level whilst away from paid employment. Departments are also able to offer up to five years' unpaid leave to staff wishing to take a career break for domestic reasons. Training is offered to help women managers gain the skills and confidence needed to progress to senior levels of the Service.

Among new Civil Service entrants in 1989, 59 per cent were female. Some 46 per cent of new appointments in the mainstream management grade at Executive Officer level were women. Women also accounted for 41 per cent of new entrants to the fast stream administrative grades; 27 per cent in the science group; and 11 per cent in the professional and tech-

nology group. Some 6 per cent of civil servants in the top
three grades of the service were women compared with 4 per
cent in 1984; 10 per cent of Grade 5 staff (8 per cent in 1986)
and 11 per cent of Grade 7 staff (8 per cent in 1986) were
women.

Career Development

Women are concentrated in the lower layers of the Civil Service
as a result of higher resignation rates and lower promotion rates
among women up to Senior Executive Officer level. Several
factors contribute to the lower promotion rates of women,
including the attitude of promotion board members, the use of
long seniority requirements at the initial stage of the promotion
process and the relative scarcity of women on some promotion
boards.

Departments provide training and guidance for promotion
board members on avoiding discrimination. New guidance has
been issued encouraging departments to avoid the use of
seniority in selecting candidates wherever possible. Departments have been successful in recruiting women as promotion
board members for the more junior grades, but there are still
problems in finding women qualified to serve on boards for
more senior and specialist staff.

Access to training is another important factor in career
development and departments are recommended to ensure that
staff with domestic responsibilities have access to training. In
1989, 21 departments ran women-only management development training courses, compared with eight in 1987. In
addition, a group of departments is taking steps to meet the
needs of staff with domestic responsibilities. For example, they

are introducing an interdepartmental approach to training for junior managers and reducing the time that participants have to spend away from home. The group is also developing re-entry training for people returning from career breaks.

The Civil Service believes that it is important that women should participate in departmental management development programmes. Although they comprise less than 11 per cent of staff in Grades 4 to 7, nearly 18 per cent of staff in the senior management development programme for these grades are women.

Sexual Harassment

Departments are required to ensure that staff are aware that sexual harassment at work is not tolerated and of procedures for dealing with complaints. By January 1990, 29 departments had issued specific policy statements and guidance on sexual harassment, and ten had nominated women contact officers.

Maternity and Paternity Leave

Paid maternity leave provision has been increased from 13 to 14 weeks and a new entitlement of two days' paternity leave has been introduced. Civil Service maternity leave and special leave rules now make it possible to take 48 weeks' maternity leave, including 14 on full pay, followed by up to five years' unpaid leave.

Training

Official bodies responsible for training in Britain adhere to the principle of equal opportunities for men and women. They encourage the provision of training to help women who want to enter or return to work, to move into employment areas traditionally dominated by men and to overcome past inequalities. Training programmes of special interest to women include single-sex courses, part-time and flexible-hours training, and open learning. Lone parents in training can obtain help with the costs of childcare under the Government's Employment Training programme (for the longer-term unemployed); some 70,000 women are on the Employment Training programme. Both Employment Training and Youth Training (offering planned work experience and training for 16- and 17-year-olds) are open to either sex; in 1990, 38 per cent of trainees on Youth Training were girls.

Many training institutions, including further education colleges, run 'Wider Opportunities for Women' courses under the Employment Training programme. The courses are for women who have decided to return to work after a period at home, and are designed to overcome specific problems, such as lack of confidence, out-of-date skills, lack of knowledge of the labour market and job application techniques, and the difficulties of combining the demands of work and family. Their main target is unskilled and unqualified women, who are likely to face the greatest problems when going back to work, but there are also courses for women returning to managerial or supervisory jobs and occupations using new technology. 'Back to the Future', a recent BBC radio project supported by the Government, aimed to help women to return to work through the use of a telephone 'helpline', exhibitions and conferences.

Another initiative, funded by the Department of Employment, is the Women in Technology scheme, run by the Open

University (see p. 32). Under the scheme, women wishing to go back to work as technologists are helped to follow courses in electronics, microprocessing, telecommunications, design and computing. The Department of Employment is also broadening opportunities for women to train for jobs involving high skill or high responsibility through special grant and scholarship schemes, and it funds research into problems facing women employed at these levels.

The Technician Engineering Scholarship Scheme provides training over two years for unemployed women aged 18 to 25. It leads to a Higher National Certificate in Electronics and Software Engineering; over 200 women have joined the scheme since it began. Under the Women and Technician Training Scheme, women employed in unskilled and semi-skilled jobs are retrained to become technicians or technician engineers. Both schemes are supported by the Department of Employment and the Engineering Industry Training Board. The Engineering Council runs a Women Into Science and Engineering scheme to encourage girls and women to consider science and engineering as careers.

In 1989–90 the Department of Employment supported 42 higher-level courses for women only. These varied from short courses for professional women returners, to one-year postgraduate courses. The main areas of training were engineering, information technology, business studies and management. Up to £440,000 has been made available by the Government for projects aimed at encouraging women to develop information technology skills as part of the Women into Information Technology campaign launched in March 1990.

Vocational training provision for women has benefited

from Britain's membership of the European Community: it is estimated that roughly one-third of funding received by Britain under the Community's European Social Fund for vocational training and retraining projects has directly assisted women workers. The Fund supports projects exclusively for women such as the unemployed, or those returning to work after caring for a family. The European Women's Training Network—IRIS, a Brussels-based network—has 34 training projects in Britain.

Mary Wollstonecraft (1759–97), educationalist and writer, is considered by many to be the first major feminist. She was the author of *A Vindication of the Rights of Women.*

Fashion designer Vivienne Westwood has been surprising
the fashion world with her exotic creations since the late
1970s, when she introduced the 'punk' look.

Yve Newbold was appointed company secretary of
Hanson PLC, one of Britain's largest firms, in 1986.
Mrs Newbold, who has four grown-up children, is
a non-executive director of British Telecom and a
governor of the of the London Business School.

Patricia Scotland became Britain's first black woman Queen's Counsel in April 1991. QCs are senior barristers who were originally appointed to represent the Crown in court cases.

Annie Lennox, Scottish-born singer with one of Britain's most successful rock bands, the Eurythmics.

BBC television news reporter Kate Adie interviewing Brigadier Cordingley, commander of the 'Desert Rats'— Britain's 8th Army regiment—during the Gulf War.

Christine Crawley, Labour Member of the European Parliament for Birmingham East. The European Parliament has a proportionately larger British female representation (11 out of 81) than the House of Commons (44 out of 650).

Young women are increasingly taking up formerly all-male team sports like football, rugby and cricket. Their popularity is likely to spread even further with the advent of television coverage.

Dame Judi Dench, internationally acclaimed stage actress, seen as Gertrude in the National Theatre's 1989 production of *Hamlet*.

Elizabeth Symons, leader of the First Division Association, the trade union for senior civil servants.

Crimewriter P. D. James holding a copy of *Devices and Desires* which, in common with several other of her novels, has been adapted for television.

The Government believes that much greater numbers of women should be persuaded to enter traditionally male-dominated occupations such as engineering. It has introduced a broad and balanced school curriculum which requires both girls and boys to study science and mathematics up to the age of 16.

The Department of Employment and the engineering industry sponsor numerous training courses for women wishing to enter or re-enter the job market as technologists.

British Airways pilots on the flight deck of a Boeing 747. The airline currently has around 30 women pilots on its staff.

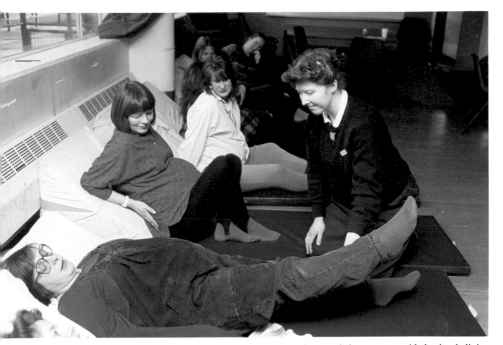

Antenatal classes are provided at local clinics under the National Health Service. Working women have a legal right to visit antenatal clinics during working hours.

A selection of information material from the Equal Opportunities Commission, which works towards eliminating discrimination against women and promotes equality of opportunity.

An advice session at one of the 1,300 Citizens Advice Bureaux (CABs) throughout Britain, which offer advice on state and voluntary services as well as housing and legal matters. Women make up over three-quarters of CAB paid and voluntary workers.

A mobile cervical cancer screening unit. A nationwide screening programme aims to reduce deaths from cancer of the cervix by inviting all women aged 20 to 64 to be screened regularly.

Social Welfare

HEALTH CARE

Since 1986 women's health has been specifically identified within the responsibilities of a minister at the Department of Health. Ministers regularly meet representatives from the National Council of Women (see p. 70) and other women's groups to discuss women's health issues. The Department is represented on the Women's Health Forum of the Health Education Authority, a body within the National Health Service (NHS) responsible for health education. It currently funds over 30 voluntary organisations and charities concerned with women's health, such as the Maternity Alliance, the Women's National Cancer Control Campaign and Women's Health Concern.

In addition to the general range of health services appropriate to both sexes, certain services within the NHS are needed to meet the specific requirements of women. In 1987 Britain became the first country in the European Community to launch a nationwide breast cancer screening programme, and in 1988 a comprehensive cervical cancer screening service (see p. 53).

Parents and Children

Special preventive services are made available under the NHS to safeguard the health of expectant mothers and mothers with young children. Services comprise free dental treatment, dried milk and vitamins; health education for parents before and after childbirth; and vaccination and immunisation of children against infectious diseases. Pregnant women receive antenatal care from their family doctor and hospital clinics, and women in paid employment have the right to visit the clinics during working hours. Some 99 per cent of women have their babies in hospital, returning home shortly afterwards to be attended by a midwife or health visitor and, where necessary, a family doctor.

The Government attaches great importance to improving the quality of maternity services, and to making them more sensitive to the needs and wishes of mothers and their families. Between 1978 and 1988 the maternal death rate in England and Wales decreased from 0·11 to 0·06 per 1,000 total births. The perinatal mortality rate (the number of stillbirths and deaths in the first week of life) has fallen in Britain from 15·6 per 1,000 births in 1979 to 8·3 per 1,000 births in 1989; the infant mortality rate (deaths of live-born infants under one year of age) fell from 13·3 per 1,000 in 1979 to 8·4 per 1,000 in 1989. These are the lowest figures ever recorded. A draft European Community directive on the protection of pregnant women at work is being considered by the British Government and other interested parties.

Human Fertilisation and Embryology

The world's first 'test-tube baby' was born in Britain in 1978, as a result of the technique of *in vitro* fertilisation. This opened up new horizons for helping with problems of infertility and for the science of embryology. The social, ethical and legal implications were examined by a committee of inquiry under Baroness Warnock. Reporting in 1984, the committee concluded that certain specialised forms of infertility treatment, including artificial insemination by donor and *in vitro* fertilisation, were ethically acceptable, but recommended that surrogate motherhood (the practice whereby one woman bears a child for another) organised by commercial agencies should be prohibited. Subject to strict controls, research on human embryos was considered acceptable, but only up to the fourteenth day after fertilisation. The committee concluded that a licensing authority should be established to regulate infertility services and research (see Further Reading). Legislation to ban commercial surrogacy agencies, and advertising of, or for, surrogacy services, was passed in 1985.

The Human Fertilisation and Embryology Act 1990 implements the main recommendations of the Warnock report, including the setting up of a licensing authority to regulate certain infertility treatments, and the strict regulation of human embryo research. The Act also provides for the status of children born as a result of such treatments, and clarifies the position on surrogacy where contracts are not legally enforceable. These provisions constitute one of the most comprehensive pieces of legislation on assisted reproduction and embryo research in the world.

Family Planning

Free family planning facilities are available from family doctors and from health authority family planning clinics. Voluntary agencies complement NHS services. Family planning services are provided to under-16s where parental consent has been granted, and in exceptional circumstances without parental consent.

Abortion

Abortion is regulated by the Abortion Act 1967, which was amended in 1990 to introduce a time limit of 24 weeks for the majority of abortions. The Act allows the ending of pregnancy by a doctor if two doctors consider that the risk of injury to the physical or mental health of the pregnant woman, or children of her family, would be greater if the pregnancy continued than if it were ended. An abortion on these grounds is to be allowed if the woman is not more than 24 weeks pregnant. An abortion may also be allowed, without a time limit, if two doctors consider that it is necessary to prevent grave permanent injury to the health of the woman; that the continuance of the pregnancy would involve risk to life of the woman greater than if the pregnancy were ended; or where there is substantial risk that if the child were born it would be seriously handicapped.

Abortions are carried out in NHS hospitals or in private premises approved for the purpose by the Government. Over half of the legal abortions to women resident in England and Wales in 1989 were performed in private hospitals and clinics; in Scotland, 97 per cent of abortions take place in NHS hospitals.

The Act does not apply in Northern Ireland.

AIDS

The Government remains concerned by the threat of AIDS to women as well as men. At the end of June 1991, 266 cases of AIDS in women had been reported. There were 1,807 reports of women who were HIV antibody positive. The Department of Health has provided funding to health authorities for local AIDS co-ordinators whose role includes liaising with local voluntary and statutory organisations in order to develop policy and a joint strategy for HIV prevention. This includes identifying gaps in provisions for specific groups, such as women. The Department has also funded 'Positively Women', a voluntary organisation for women who are HIV positive.

The Health Education Authority, which is responsible for the Government's AIDS public education campaign, promotes programmes aimed at the general population, and specific groups in society, to increase awareness of the dangers of HIV infection and AIDS, and of how the public can protect itself. Women are identified as a key group, and the Authority has developed materials specifically aimed at young, sexually active women.

The Authority has supported the development of a Women's Health Network which has produced a database containing a directory of women's health initiatives. The Network is also identifying training needs in relation to HIV and AIDS health promotion work; carrying out pilot projects directed at youth groups and women's organisations; and providing further education access courses for women.

Smoking

Smoking is the major cause of preventable illness and death in Britain. Mortality from lung cancer among women has been rising in recent years and, as a result, specific measures aimed at women have been taken. The Health Education Authority offers advice on giving up smoking and in 1989 a major campaign was launched to discourage smoking among teenagers, particularly teenage girls. In February 1991 the Government announced that it would fund an extensive campaign to persuade women to stop smoking during pregnancy.

The current voluntary agreement with the tobacco industry on tobacco promotion prohibits advertising in magazines where a third or more of the readers are young women. One of six health warnings, required to be printed on cigarette packets and related advertising by the voluntary agreement, draws attention to the damage that smoking during pregnancy can do to an unborn baby.

Misuse of Drugs and Alcohol

The growth of drug misuse among women, including pregnant women and women with young children, is a matter of increasing concern. Injecting drugs with shared equipment has been the major cause of known infection of AIDS among women in Great Britain. In some cases the infection has been passed on to these women's babies.

In 1986 the Government issued guidelines to health authorities on the development of drug misuse services, and clinics have been set up in Glasgow and Birmingham and several other areas. It is encouraging the development of co-operative working between the various agencies providing services for women drug misusers.

The Government acknowledges that there is a high rate of prescribing of tranquillisers to women, which can lead to dependence. Advice and counselling services for drug misusers also offer help to tranquilliser dependants. Many of these services have been established with pump-priming grants from the Government, or with funds made available to health authorities specifically for the development of such services.

The far-reaching effects of alcohol misuse in terms of illness, family breakdown, inefficiency at work, loss of earnings, accidents and crime are widely recognised. Although women drink less than men and suffer less alcohol-related harm, they now show a greater rate of increase both in consumption and in the incidence of harm. The Government believes that the reduction of alcohol misuse requires a range of action by central and local government, voluntary and community bodies, the health professions, business and trade unions. It places emphasis on policies to prevent alcohol misuse and continues to seek better information about the causes of problem drinking. It also aims to encourage healthier life-styles, and to provide help for the problem drinker at an early stage.

Problem drinkers may be helped by primary health care teams—general practitioners, nurses and social workers; by counselling and advice centres; and treatment and rehabilitation facilities run by health authorities or voluntary organisations. Increasingly, services are being provided specially for women.

In 1987 the Government formed an interdepartmental ministerial group to develop strategy for combating the misuse of alcohol. Measures taken include legislative changes, as well as steps to secure better health education and more effective action by local services and organisations. Legislation came into force in 1988 to strengthen the law banning the sale of alcohol to people under 18 years. At the same time, stricter controls on alcohol advertising were introduced. People appearing in advertisements must now be seen to be over 25 years of age; excessive drinking is not to be encouraged, shown or implied; and alcohol is not to be advertised alongside aggressive or anti-social behaviour. Alcohol must not be shown as increasing competence, attractiveness or prowess. Independent television has restricted the advertising of alcohol in television pro-grammes aimed at young people.

In 1989 the Government announced increased funding for the Health Education Authority's alcohol education pro-gramme. This aims to reduce the harm caused by the misuse of alcohol by promoting sensible drinking as part of a healthy way of life. It also seeks to develop a climate of opinion which favours appropriate measures to prevent alcohol-related harm. Alcohol misuse co-ordinators have been appointed in each of the 14 regional health authorities with the aim of developing strategies to counter the misuse of alcohol.

The Department of Health is funding MIND, the leading voluntary body in the mental health field, to establish a national directory of services for tranquilliser dependants and the pro-duction of up-to-date publicity material. It has made funds available to Alcohol Concern, a national voluntary organisation, to improve counselling and advisory services and has made provision for grants to be paid to local authorities to cover costs incurred by voluntary organisations catering for people with alcohol or drug problems. The Department has also financed the voluntary organisation DAWN (Drugs, Alcohol, Women, Now) to undertake a survey of the needs of women drug misusers and problem drinkers.

Cancer Screening

The cervical screening programme is designed to reduce deaths from cancer of the cervix by inviting women to be screened regularly, so as to identify and treat conditions that might otherwise develop into cancer. Every district health authority in England has had computerised call and recall systems since 1988, which enable all women aged between 20 and 64 to be called regularly for cervical cancer screening. Similar arrangements apply in Wales, Scotland and Northern Ireland. Between 1978 and 1988, deaths from cervical cancer in England and Wales fell by 10 per cent to under 2,000 a year; the death rate per million women aged 20 to 74 dropped by 16 per cent.

The Government is in the process of setting up a nationwide breast cancer screening service for all women aged between 50 and 64. The service is now in operation in most areas, and all eligible women in England and Wales should have received their screening invitations by 1993 (and in Scotland and Northern Ireland by 1994).

Female Medical Staff

The Government is keen to increase the numbers of female medical staff, both in the interests of women who choose to make a career in this field, and in recognition of the fact that it can be very important for some women, for example, those from some ethnic minority communities, to have access to treatment by female medical staff. The proportion of female medical students has risen steadily to almost 50 per cent of the total, and this will be increasingly reflected in the proportion of women doctors.

A government report on issues affecting women doctors recommends that there should be more female doctors in the higher grades of the profession. Part-time training for senior registrars is already in operation and there will be a scheme to improve part-time training opportunities available to registrars. Guidance on equal opportunities in appointment procedures will be issued to health authorities. In 1987 an initiative called 'Achieving a Balance' was introduced with the aim of eliminating career 'bottlenecks' affecting both male and female doctors.

SOCIAL SECURITY

Originally, Britain's social security system was aimed at providing basic maintenance benefits tailored to the presumed circumstances of the individual according to sex, age and marital status. Hence, it overtly treated men and women differently and had a special set of provisions for married women. The past 20 years have seen extensive changes in the scheme, which have moved it away from a system of protection for married women based largely on rights derived from their husbands' insurance, to one where women are increasingly building up their own rights to contributory benefits and have gained access to most non-contributory benefits on the same terms as men.

So far as differences in treatment remain, they tend to favour women in recognising the needs of older women who have not contributed in the past and who rely on their husbands' insurance records for protection in old age, and of those who planned their lives around the current female pension age.

Benefits are increased annually, the uprating being linked to rises in retail prices. The rates given are those effective from April 1991 to April 1992.

The rising divorce rate and increase in births outside marriage have led to a growth in the number of lone-parent families, which now comprise about one-sixth of all families with children. Nine out of ten lone parents are women, as are three-quarters of carers of elderly, sick and disabled people. Many lone-parent families and carers depend to a lesser or greater extent on social security benefits.

Mothers and Children

Under the statutory maternity pay scheme, women leaving employment to have a baby receive maternity pay directly from their employer. To qualify, a woman must have worked for the same employer for at least 26 weeks up to and including the fifteenth week before the week her baby is due, and have had average weekly earnings in the last eight weeks of that period which are not less than the lower earnings limit for National Insurance contributions. Statutory maternity pay is normally paid for 18 weeks. There are two rates: where a woman has been working full-time for the same employer for at least two years, or part-time for the same employer for a minimum of five years, she is entitled to 90 per cent of her average weekly earnings for the first six weeks and to the lower rate of £44·50 for the remaining 12 weeks. If a woman has been employed for between six months and two years, she is entitled to payments for the full 18 weeks at the lower rate.

Women who are self-employed, have recently changed jobs or given up their job, and are therefore ineligible for maternity pay, may be eligible for a weekly maternity allowance of £40·60 which is payable for 18 weeks. To qualify for this, a woman must have been employed or self-employed and paid standard rate National Insurance contributions for at least 26 of the 52 weeks ending 15 weeks before the baby is expected.

A payment of £100 from the social fund is available to those on low incomes for each living child born or for a stillborn child if the pregnancy lasts for at least 28 weeks. It is also payable for an adopted baby if the mother or her partner are receiving income support or family credit (see p. 57).

Child benefit of £8·25 a week for a first child and £7·25 for each of the other children is payable for virtually all children and payment is normally made to the mother.[1] The benefit does not depend on payment of contributions, nor is it income-related or subject to tax. It is payable for children under 16 and for those aged 16, 17 or 18 continuing in full-time education.[2] In addition, lone parent benefit of £5·60 a week is payable to certain lone parents and other people bringing up children on their own. A non-contributory guardian's allowance of £10·70 a week is available to a person entitled to child benefit for a child whose parents have both died. In certain limited circumstances it can be paid on the death of only one parent.

[1] From October 1991 the rates will be £9·25 and £7·50 respectively.
[2] Up to and including GCE Advanced level and its equivalents.

From April 1993 a new Child Support Agency will be responsible for tracing absent parents and for assessing, collecting and enforcing child-maintenance payments.

Income Support

Income support is payable to people who are not in work, or who work for less than 24 hours a week, and whose financial resources are below set levels. It consists of a personal allowance ranging from £23·65 for a single person or lone parent aged under 18, to £62·25 for a couple, at least one of whom is aged 18 or over. There are additional personal allowances for children and premiums for families, lone parents, pensioners, long-term sick and disabled people and carers. Partners decide which of them should claim.

Family Credit

Family credit is payable to working families on modest incomes with children. The amount payable depends on a family's income and the number and ages of the children in the family. A maximum rate, consisting of an adult rate of £38·30 a week plus an age-related rate for each child, is payable when the net income does not exceed £62·25 a week. The rate is then reduced by 70 pence for each pound by which net income exceeds this amount.

The scheme favours women to the extent that in a two-parent family the benefit is paid to the woman, and because more than a third of those receiving family credit are lone parents, the great majority of them women. Lone-parent families receive the same amount of benefit as two-parent families.

Social Fund

Discretionary payments, in the form of loans or grants, are made available to people on low incomes who have special or emergency needs. Payments are also made from the social fund to help with the costs of maternity, or of funerals, or with heating during very cold weather. These latter payments are entitlements and are not subject to the same budgetary considerations as other social fund payments.

Widows

All widows receive a tax-free single payment of £1,000 following the death of their husbands, provided that their husbands had paid a minimum number of National Insurance contributions. A widowed mother with a young family receives a widowed mother's weekly allowance of £52·00 with a further £9·70 for the first child and £10·70 for each subsequent child if her late husband had satisfied certain contribution conditions. A widow's pension of £52·00 a week is payable to a widow who is 45 years or over when her husband dies, or when her entitlement to widowed mother's allowance ends. Payment continues until the widow remarries or begins to draw retirement pension. Women whose husbands have died as a result of an industrial injury or disease may also qualify, regardless of whether their husbands had paid National Insurance contributions.

A man whose wife dies when both are over pension age inherits his wife's pension rights just as a widow inherits her husband's rights.

State Retirement Pension

A state retirement pension is payable to women at the age of 60 and to men at the age of 65. The Sex Discrimination Act 1986 (see p. 22) protects employees of different sexes in a particular occupation from being required to retire at different ages. This, however, has not affected the payment of state retirement pensions at different ages for men and women. The state pension scheme consists of a basic weekly pension of £52 for a single person and £83·25 for a married couple, together with an additional earnings-related pension.

Rights to basic pensions are safeguarded for mothers who are away from paid employment looking after children and for people giving up paid employment to care for severely disabled relatives. Women contributors receive the same basic pension as men with the same earnings, provided that they have paid full-rate National Insurance contributions when working.

Occupational Pension Schemes

The 1986 European Community directive, applying the principle of equal treatment to occupational schemes, has been incorporated into British law with the additional requirement that schemes 'contracted out' of the State Earnings-Related Pension Scheme must make provision for widowers' as well as widows' pensions. From January 1993 schemes will not be able to discriminate between men and women. The State Earnings Related Additional Pension, which is obligatory for employed people without contracted-out occupational or personal pensions, makes no distinction between men and women, and either spouse can inherit a deceased spouse's pension rights.

Following a ruling of the European Court of Justice in 1990, occupational schemes must have an equal pension age for men and women. However, the ruling did not apply to statutory social schemes and the state pension will continue to be paid to men at 65 and women at 60.

Developments

In the last few years several developments in the social security field have benefited women:

—all women can now claim for a partner on the same terms as men under the income support scheme, the housing benefit scheme (which offers help with the costs of rents to people on low incomes) and the community charge benefit scheme (which offsets the cost to low-income individuals and families of the new local taxes);

—severe disablement allowance is payable to men and women on equal terms and the invalid care allowance, which is paid to the carer rather than the invalid, was made available to married women on the same basis as single women and men in 1986;

—from October 1990 a carer premium of £10 (£10·80 from April 1991) a week has been offered as a new income support, housing benefit or community charge benefit premium for carers of disabled people.

PERSONAL SOCIAL SERVICES

Child Care

Day care facilities for children under five are supplied by local authorities, voluntary agencies and privately. In allocating places in their day nurseries and other facilities, local authorities give priority to children from families with special social or health needs. Local authorities also register childminders, private day nurseries and playgroups in their areas and provide support and advice services for them.

The Government recognises that family responsibilities can be a barrier to women returning to work and pursuing careers. It also believes that women suffer the disadvantages of interrupted careers, and on returning to work may have less demanding, lower-grade work. In 1990 it announced that the value of childcare facilities provided by employers would cease to be treated as employee-income for income tax purposes. The Ministerial Group on Women's Issues has given priority to drawing together the work of government departments already done to promote high quality childcare. In 1989 it agreed a five-point plan which has already been implemented. This covers:

—improvements to the registration and enforcement arrangements for day nurseries, childminders and play groups;

—further encouragement to employers to use tax reliefs on childcare facilities;

—guidance to local education authorities and schools, encouraging the use of school premises for after-school and holiday schemes;

—further initial support for the voluntary sector; and

—a voluntary accreditation scheme to supply information about the availability and quality of childcare facilities.

The Ministerial Group approved a follow-up programme of action in February 1990. This comprises:

—issuing new guidance and regulations to local authorities on day care services for children;

—helping to improve local authority practice on the registration of day care services;

—encouraging the development of information services on childcare for both parents and employers;

—continuing to encourage employers to become involved in helping staff with childcare; and

—continuing to set an example to employers by developing a range of flexible working patterns and childcare facilities for civil servants choosing to combine paid work and family responsibilities (see below).

Government as Employer

The 1984 programme of action recognised that lack of childcare facilities was a barrier to women's employment. It recommended that departments should consider proposals for day care schemes and, in particular, encourage and offer practical help in organising holiday playschemes. Staff from the Office of the Minister for the Civil Service work with departments and agencies in developing childcare provision. Departments and agencies are allowed to support childcare schemes where value for money can be demonstrated. Guidance on setting up nurseries and holiday play schemes is being revised for circulation to departments and agencies. Seminars on child care are arranged to facilitate the spread of best practice.

The Government has made significant progress as an employer in providing childcare facilities. Departments and agencies are currently operating one sponsored childminding scheme, three advice/referral projects and 85 holiday play-schemes.

There are now 19 nurseries for the children of civil servants, and feasibility studies on nursery care are being carried out at several other locations. Government departments also take up places in nurseries operated by other employers and private contractors.

Private Sector

Private sector employers are showing growing interest in assisting employees with childcare. Some, the Midland Bank and Glaxo (Britain's largest pharmaceuticals group), for instance, are opening nurseries and crèche facilities for employees' children, while others are helping through financial payments or by giving their employees 'childcare vouchers'. The Midland Bank uses up to 100 nurseries (three of them belonging to the Bank) for children under five and it plans to set up holiday playschemes for workers' school-children. Glaxo plans to open three nurseries catering for 150 children close to company sites. It is also to provide childminders in an effort to retain female scientific and medical staff. BP intends to set up a 50-place nursery at its new headquarters in London. Rolls-Royce has established a scheme to care for workers' children at its Derby factory, before and after school hours and in the school holidays. ICL, Rank Xerox and the F.I. Group all operate working practices using new technology to enable women to pursue full-time careers from home.

Care of Elderly and Disabled People

Three-quarters of unpaid family carers are women, typically wives, daughters or daughters-in-law of the person being cared for. Services which help to relieve the burdens of women caring for elderly or disabled relatives include home helps, sitters-in, laundry services, meals on wheels services, day centres and clubs. Many of the services are provided by voluntary agencies in which women themselves play a significant role.

Support Services for Women

Advice and help for women with problems is available through local authorities or from several voluntary organisations. There are many refuges for women, many of whom have young children, whose home conditions become intolerable and who have nowhere else to go. The refuges offer short-term accommodation and support while a solution to the problem is worked out.

Women and Criminal Justice

Police Recruitment and Training

Women have equal opportunities for appointment to the police service, and all recruits must satisfy standard entry requirements and undergo the same initial training. Women officers are deployed on the full range of police duties. Further specialised training is related to the duties on which the officer may be employed and, within individual police forces, women officers may receive specialised training in subjects such as domestic violence, child abuse and sexual assault. The recruitment and career development of women within individual police forces are regularly monitored.

Custodial Establishments

Male and female custodial establishments in England and Wales operate in general under the same policies and statutory rules. There are, however, exceptions which reflect female inmates' special needs. The provision of specialist accommodation and staff to look after pregnant women and babies is one example. Also, treatment of male and female juvenile offenders differs. Unlike juvenile males, females under 17 years of age may not in any circumstances be held in a prison or remand centre while awaiting trial. Whereas boys of 14 can be sentenced to a term in a young offenders' institution, girl offenders must be 15 before receiving such sentences. The Government is considering abolishing all custodial sentences for girls aged 15 to 17.

The Prison Service has considered the particular problems of mothers in prison by commissioning research into the physical and psychological development of babies in prison compared with those not subject to this experience. Broadly, this concluded that residence in a mother and baby unit did not significantly impair the development of babies. However, the research did identify areas where there is scope for the development of better childcare practice, and these are now being addressed. Independent inspections by childcare experts in the Department of Health help to monitor progress. The probation service tries to find suitable community service work for female offenders, especially for pregnant women and women with young children, as an alternative to prison.

Violence Against Women

There is a comprehensive body of law on sexual offences. Maximum penalties for attempted rape and indecent assault against women have recently been substantially increased in England and Wales; in Scotland these crimes can be punished by life imprisonment. Guidance given by the Government to chief constables on the investigation of sexual assault stresses the need for sensitivity and tact in the treatment of victims, and encourages chief constables to keep training needs under constant review.

Legislation relating to domestic violence provides the right to apply for an injunction, personal protection orders, or exclusion orders to deal with this problem. In Scotland, the Matrimonial Homes (Family Protection) (Scotland) Act 1981 strengthened the law on matrimonial interdicts (similar to exclusion orders) and made new provision in relation to the rights of occupancy of spouses in a matrimonial home. Revised guidelines to the police in Scotland about the provisions of the Act stress, among other things, that the safety of the aggrieved woman and her family should be of paramount concern to the police.

Compensation is available from public funds for the victims of violent crime. Practical advice and emotional support are provided by victim support schemes and rape crisis centres. These voluntary schemes receive financial assistance from central government under a variety of programmes.

The Ministerial Group on Women's Issues has considered the issue of domestic violence in the context of a Home Office research study on the subject and a report of the Women's National Commission (see Further Reading). The Group set in hand further work in 1989 on the use of the criminal and civil law, and the response to domestic violence made by the police, the Crown Prosecution Service and the courts. It has also commissioned a review of the way in which social services departments and health services could give more effective help to victims of domestic violence, especially in the early stages. Consideration is being given to the role of personal and social education of schoolchildren in helping to prevent domestic violence; guidance for schools is being examined.

The Department of Health provides funds to the Women's Aid Federation (England) to support a network of women's refuges (see p. 64); there are similar arrangements in Wales, Scotland and Northern Ireland.

The Law Commission is carrying out a review of the law in England and Wales relating to domestic violence, including rape within marriage; in Scotland a man can already be charged with the rape of his wife.

Prostitution

Under the Sexual Offences Act 1956, it is an offence in England and Wales for a man knowingly to live on the earnings of prostitution, and it is an offence for a woman to exercise control, direction or influence over a prostitute's movements by assisting or compelling her to engage in prostitution. It is also an offence to procure a woman to become a prostitute in any part of the world.

The Sexual Offences Act 1985 makes 'kerbcrawling' a specific offence in England and Wales. Broadly, it is unlawful for a man to solicit a woman for the purpose of prostitution, from or near a motor vehicle. It is also an offence for a man on foot persistently to solicit a woman in a street or public place. Thus, for the first time under British law, male clients of female prostitutes are liable to prosecution in certain circumstances.

Similar legal provisions on prostitution apply in Scotland.

Pornography

A number of legal measures have been introduced to tighten up the law relating to pornography. The Protection of Children Act 1978 is designed to prevent the exploitation of children in connection with indecent photographs and films. The Indecent Displays (Control) Act 1981 prohibits the display of indecent material in a public place, or where it can be seen from a public place. The Cinematography (Amendment) Act 1982, now subsumed in the Cinema Act 1985, brought bogus cinema clubs within the scope of the licensing arrangements for cinemas. The Local Government (Miscellaneous Provisions) Act 1982 contains provisions enabling local authorities in England and Wales to control the number and location of sex shops by means of a licensing scheme. The Civic Government (Scotland) Act 1982 provides for the control of sex shops and the displaying of obscene material. The Video Recordings Act 1984 prohibits the supply, offer to supply, or possession for supply, of unclassified material in video form.

The Government has indicated that it will continue to keep the law under close review and will consider further legislation.

Women's Organisations

There are hundreds of women's organisations in Britain covering the voluntary sector, political parties, religious groupings, trade unions, single-issue pressure groups and the professions. Some aim to improve the quality of life for women in the home by offering opportunities for social and cultural activities. Others seek to change the status of women in the political, economic, public, legal and social spheres. Certain organisations campaign on issues of particular importance to women, such as abortion, or represent the interests of a particular group of women, for example, teachers. Many have international interests and maintain links with similar bodies overseas.

Several organisations have many affiliates and act as umbrella groups for women's organisations. The largest are the National Council of Women (set up in 1985) with 90 affiliates, and the newly formed National Alliance of Women's Organisations with 176 affiliates.

Of the broad-based organisations for women, the biggest are the National Federation of Women's Institutes (founded in 1915) with 325,000 members, the National Union of Townswomen's Guilds (1929) with 120,000 members, the Mothers' Union (1876) with 188,000 members and the Women's Royal Voluntary Service (1938) with 160,000 members. These and many others are national in scope and have branches in all parts of Britain.

Women's Institutes aim to provide education for women in subjects such as citizenship, public affairs, music and drama; they also give instruction in agriculture, handicrafts, home economics and social welfare, and seek to promote international understanding. The Mothers' Union, which forms a part of the Anglican Church, works to promote Christian family life through its departments for education, young families, social concern and overseas affairs, and through prayer groups. Other religious organisations include the National Board of Catholic Women, the League of Jewish Women, and the National Free Church Women's Council.

Organisations representing the interests of specific groups include the National Association of Widows, the Carers' National Association, and Gingerbread (representing lone parents). The 300 Group, founded in 1980, aims to ensure that more women (at least 300) are elected to Parliament. It seeks to identify the special problems faced by women in entering politics and to support their efforts.

The Fawcett Society, founded in 1866, strives for the acceptance of equal status for women in the home and in public life, and equal educational and job opportunities. It also runs the Fawcett Library, Britain's main library and archive on the history of the women's movement.

Apart from their activities in such organisations and their role as carers women play a particularly active role in voluntary bodies open to both sexes, and are particularly concerned with areas of social welfare such as health and handicap. A recent government-commissioned study found that 25 per cent of women were doing voluntary work, compared with 21 per cent of men.

The International Context

Britain has played a full part in the formulation of policies relating to the status of women in international forums such as the United Nations, the European Community, the Council of Europe and the Commonwealth. It seeks wherever possible to implement the policies adopted by them.

United Nations

The United Nations Decade for Women (1976–85) was launched following International Women's Year in 1975. The aim of the Decade, whose broad themes were equality, development and peace, was to stimulate national and international action to solve those problems of social and economic development which place women in a less favourable position than men. In 1980 a conference took place in Copenhagen to mark the mid-point of the Decade, at which three sub-themes—employment, health and education—were introduced.

To mark the end of the Decade for Women, a conference was held in Nairobi in 1985. In response to the *Forward-Looking Strategies for the Advancement of Women to the Year 2000* agreed at the conference, a review of British government policies for the advancement of women was published in 1987. The review set out the extent to which the goals and objectives of the strategies were already being met in Britain and covered such areas as matrimonial and family law, employment, health,

education, industry, science and technology, social security and
the criminal justice system (see Further Reading).

Britain has ratified the United Nations Convention on the
Elimination of All Forms of Discrimination against Women,
adopted by the UN General Assembly in 1979. In January 1990
the Ministerial Group on Women's Issues presented the British
Government's initial report on the implementation of the
Convention in Britain. Britain has acceded to the 1952 Convention on the Political Rights of Women.

European Community
The Treaty of Rome specifies that women should receive the
same pay as men. Three European Community directives deal
with equal treatment of women: equal pay (implemented by
the Equal Pay Act 1970); equal treatment in employment,
vocational training and promotion and working conditions
(implemented by the employment provisions of the Sex Discrimination Acts 1975 and 1986); and social security. The
Community has also adopted, by means of a resolution signed
in 1982, an action programme on equal opportunities for
women, which has given rise to proposals for further Community measures.

Women benefit in several ways from British membership of
the Community. They receive, for example, financial help for
vocational training from the European Social Fund. Women's
affairs are regularly debated in the European Parliament.

Other Forums
A Women and Development Unit, established at the Commonwealth Secretariat in London in 1980, works to advance the

interests of women in the Commonwealth through exchanges, training programmes, research and discussion. It also helps to identify key areas for future action by governments. Other international bodies in which the status and problems of women are discussed are the Council of Europe and the Organisation for Economic Co-operation and Development. The role of women in development is an area of co-operation between member countries of the Commonwealth.

In October 1990 ministers responsible for women's affairs from 50 member countries of the Commonwealth, including Britain, met in Ottawa to discuss strategies to promote the role of women in economic development. They reviewed the Commonwealth Plan of Action on Women and Development adopted in 1987, to integrate women's concerns into national policies and to improve women's access to decision-making processes. The Plan provides measurable indicators for assessing progress on its implementation, as well as the performance of the Commonwealth Secretariat in increasing women's participation in its activities.

Appendix I:
Equal Opportunities Commission
Strategy for the 1990s

In the light of changing economic, social and demographic trends, the Equal Opportunities Commission has reassessed its role, and in 1989 launched a new strategy to promote equal opportunities. This focuses on enabling men and women to become more responsible and effective family members and employees; helping women to take advantage of the full range of training opportunities; reducing differences between men's and women's earnings, pension rights and taxation; and developing awareness that equal opportunities affect all aspects of people's working and non-working lives.

The strategy is outlined in a document published in 1989 (see Further Reading). In this, the Commission notes that the decreasing number of young people entering the labour market, coupled with inadequate past training, has led to a skills shortage. While women are well placed to alleviate this problem, the Review says that major barriers prevent them from participating fully in the job market: these include inadequate childcare provision, lack of training, unequal pay and benefits, and financial disincentives, as well as traditional assumptions about the work that men and women do and their respective roles in society. According to the Review, women already make up 42 per cent of the workforce (50 per cent in some regions). Although this proportion is likely to rise, most women, especially those from ethnic minorities or those who carry extra responsibility for family care, are still working in lower-paid, lower-status jobs offering restricted training and promotion opportunities. The Commission shares the Government's view that greater equality of opportunity between men and women can make a real contribution to continuing national prosperity.

The Commission believes that it should change its over-riding role from that of securing equal rights for women to one of achieving central national economic objectives through the implementation of effective equal opportunities practice. Hence the new strategy focuses on the task of making fully available to society the skills which women can provide. In the Commission's view, genuine equality of opportunity will come about in several ways: far-sighted employers will continue to engage in good equal opportunities practice and respond to encouragement to attract and retain skilled and experienced male and female employees, while the less enlightened ones will change only in response to laws prohibiting their discriminatory practices. The Commission plans to direct its attention to both groups.

A summary of the Review's themes and objectives is given below.

Work and the Family

The Commission considers that the combination of massive skills shortages, fewer school-leavers and increased international competition is forcing many employers to take measures to attract and retain skilled and experienced employees. The contribution to be made by women will be greater if more provision is made for family support so that there can be a choice of care for both children and elderly and dependent relatives. A number of objectives have been set by the Commission which, if met, could make men and women more effective and responsible employees and family members. First, it aims to persuade employers to offer support for working parents and other carers. It will try to establish good practice models for out-of-school care and holiday schemes for children between the ages of 5 and 13, as well as working towards achieving improved status, qualifications and training for childminders and other childcare workers. Lastly, the Commission will endeavour to enhance the status of part-time work and to attain for part-time workers pay and non-pay benefits commensurate with those of full-time workers.

Education and Training

The Commission wants women to have the full range of opportunities for training leading to different occupations. It aims to remove barriers preventing pupils from having equal access to a curriculum that broadens educational and vocational choices and guides young women towards a wider range of possible occupations. Also, it will try to increase the number of women taking job-skills, retraining, professional and management courses, and, where appropriate, extend the provision of access courses and special training programmes for women. Women returning to work after a career break will be encouraged to take up education, training and retraining opportunities.

Equal Pay

The Review states that, in spite of the Equal Pay Act 1970, women's average hourly earnings have remained at about three-quarters of those of men for the last ten years. The Commission will seek to narrow this gap substantially within five years. Its specific objectives are to establish good practice in payment structures and job evaluation schemes free of sex bias; produce a draft code of practice on equal pay; lower barriers to the recruitment and promotion of women, focusing on growth employment sectors; and secure simplification of the Sex Discrimination and Equal Pay Acts.

Fiscal Policies and Pensions

The Review notes that disincentives within the tax and social security systems continue to make it difficult for women to become independent through paid work. Furthermore, because of their unpaid family work they have less access to pensions. In order to increase fiscal and pensions equality and to remove disincentives to employment, the Commission proposes to identify and publicise inequalities in the tax and state benefit systems, and to continue to demonstrate the need for an equal state pension age and equal state, occupational and personal pension provision.

Increasing Awareness

Achieving the Commission's objectives will not be possible, it believes, unless policy-makers and the general public are aware of the issues and understand that equality of opportunity brings advantages to all men and women at work and at home. The Commission, therefore, will attempt to secure support for its objectives among policy-makers and those who influence opinion. It intends to investigate and publicise the impact of the introduction of the single European market in 1992 on women and equal opportunities. Moreover, it will try to raise awareness at grass-roots level of equal opportunities and the role of the Commission.

In addition to bringing about change through persuasion, the Commission has unique legal powers to support people, carry out investigations, and recommend changes to equality legislation. It intends to take an active, innovatory approach, using its legal and promotional powers to make equal opportunities a reality by concentrating on the themes and specific related objectives outlined above. However, it will continue to deal with complaints and questions outside these priority areas, including those concerned with sexual harassment and discrimination in social and other settings.

Appendix II:
Historical Perspective

At the beginning of the nineteenth century, women in Britain were subject to more legal, economic and social restrictions than ever before. The industrial revolution and the changes resulting from it had eliminated many of their traditional work and domestic activities. Almost the only paid occupations of that period open to educated women of limited means were those of governess or 'companion'. The main employment for less-educated women was domestic service. Women drawn into the new textile mills, factories and workshops were almost always employed in the least-skilled and lowest-paid grades of work, and were made to work long hours under conditions both degrading and detrimental to their health.

The second-class status of women at this time was due partly to direct legal discrimination such as that which did not allow women to vote, or married women to hold property. However, women's underprivileged position was also attributable to the prejudices of a social system based on the assumption of male superiority, and to the absence of redress against the exercise of such prejudices. Since then, major changes in legal status have been made by Parliament and practically all positive legal discrimination based on sex has been removed. However, the most fundamental improvements in women's lives are thought by many to have resulted not from legal reform, but from changes in social attitudes, which, though accelerated by the campaigning of liberal reformers and the effects of two world wars, are largely due to demographic change and a revolution in the pattern of family and social life.

Women Pioneers

During the nineteenth century the change in women's status resulted in part from the work of exceptional women. There were, for example, novelists such as Jane Austen, the Brontë sisters, George Eliot and Elizabeth Gaskell; the poet Elizabeth Barrett Browning; and such women as Mary Wollstonecraft and Mrs Henry Reid, both of whom wrote on the rights of women. Harriet Martineau was one of the first women writers on economics. Humanitarians included Elizabeth Fry, pioneer of prison reform; Mary Carpenter, the champion of vagrant, neglected or delinquent children; Josephine Butler, who helped unmarried mothers and prostitutes; and Louise Twining, who campaigned for better treatment of old people in work-houses. Other women fought for better industrial conditions for their sex: Emma Paterson founded the Women's Trade Union League in 1874, in the period before women were admitted to the established trade unions on the same basis as men; and Beatrice Webb played a large part in the setting-up of Trade Boards to regulate wages and conditions in the unorganised industries in which many women were employed. There were educationists: Frances Mary Buss, headmistress of the North London Collegiate School (founded 1850); Dorothea Beale, headmistress of Cheltenham Ladies' College (founded 1853); Emily Davies, whose efforts resulted in the founding of Girton College, Cambridge in 1860; and Anne Clough, first principal of Newnham College, Cambridge (founded 1875).

The first woman doctors included Elizabeth Blackwell, who was obliged to qualify in the United States, and her successors, Elizabeth Garrett Anderson and Sophia Jex Blake, who carried on the struggle to gain admission for women to the medical profession, which was finally granted in 1876. Other women pioneered the development of new professions: for example, Octavia Hill initiated a system of housing management which is still in use, and Florence Nightingale was the founder of modern nursing.

Structural Changes

By their insistence on women's diverse capabilities, women pioneers undermined a strongly held conviction that women could be of little service outside the home. By their actions they proved that, given the opportunity, women could do useful and effective work in the world at large. Circumstances strengthened their case. After the Crimean War broke out in 1854, women began to work in areas previously exclusive to men—in military hospitals overseas and in the larger retail shops at home. The invention of the telephone and the typewriter provided more occupations for them, and during the last decade of the nineteenth century women were working in commercial offices in increasing numbers. The Civil Service followed the business lead and began to employ women typists in 1888. There had been women telegraph operators in the Service since the Controller of the Post Office had taken over the telegraph system in 1870. The first woman to be appointed to a higher post in the Civil Service was an inspector of workhouse schools, who took up the post in 1873.

As education and training for employment increased, there came a demand for representation in Parliament. The first regular suffrage committee was set up in 1855 with Barbara Leigh Smith as Secretary. From the 1860s until the outbreak of the first world war in 1914, groups of women—led by Millicent Fawcett and her colleagues as well as by 'militant' suffragettes such as Emmeline Pankhurst and her daughter Christabel—worked steadily for the enfranchisement of women. This was eventually achieved in two Acts—the Representation of the People Act 1918, which granted women over the age of 30 the right to vote, and the Parliament (Qualification of Women) Act 1918, which gave women the right to be elected as members of the House of Commons. In 1928 the minimum voting age for women was lowered to 21, the same as for men.

The first world war gave women much wider opportunities to exercise their abilities. The gaps left by men who joined the armed forces were filled by women, many of whom were doing work which was completely new to them. The number of women at work rose by nearly a quarter. The greatest number were employed in industry, and out of half a million who entered the metal trade, some 90 per cent were engaged in work normally done by men. Women were also employed in public transport and in other public services, in professional and semi-professional occupations, in the police and in the Women's Land Army. In the Civil Service there were 600 women civil servants in 1914; by 1919 there were nearly 170,000, many of them in posts where they were interchangeable with men. The women's auxiliary services were formed in conjunction with the Royal Navy, the Army and the Air Force, bringing women for the first time into the military organisation of war.

Women's contribution to the war effort between 1914 and 1918 brought about a change in public opinion, which manifested itself in a variety of ways. After the war many women left industrial employment, but the practice of adapting machinery and working methods to their different skills remained, and the consequent technical developments led to an expansion in factory employment, particularly in the light metal industries, during the 1920s and 1930s. The right of entry to most professions was formally granted to women by the Sex Disqualification (Removal) Act 1919. From then on, it became increasingly a matter of course, and not of debate, that girls should be properly educated and trained for employment. They could work in one of the professions in which there were already large numbers of educated women—nursing, teaching and secretarial work; in one of the old-established professions newly opened to women; or in one of the professions (advertising, broadcasting, institutional management and auxiliary medical services) that developed during the years between the two world wars.

In public life it became normal for women to take a share of responsibility. An Act of 1907 had confirmed the right of women to be elected as county or borough councillors and in 1908 a woman mayor was appointed for the first time. Since 1919, when Lady Astor took her seat, there have always been women in the House of Commons, some of whom have reached ministerial or Cabinet rank. The first was Margaret Bondfield, Minister of Labour (and a member of the Cabinet) in 1929, when she also became the first woman Privy Counsellor.

After 1920 the whole structure of British social and family life began to change radically, with the spread of knowledge of contraceptive methods, the associated fall in the birth-rate and the development of health and social services and of labour-saving devices in the home. During the second world war, women again replaced men called up to serve in the armed forces, and thus undertook heavy, skilled or specialised jobs normally done by men. Women also served in the armed forces and civilian men and women shared common dangers. In general, moreover, war had a levelling influence which undermined prejudices underlying sex discrimination.

Though some of the immediate impact of the 1939–45 world war on the position of women was lost with the return of peacetime conditions, the social and demographic change has continued. The re-emergence of a feminist movement in the 1960s and 1970s, which has pressed for equality of treatment in a wide range of areas, was in part responsible for the passing of the Equal Pay Act 1970, the Sex Discrimination Act 1975, and more recent legislation which has removed most of the remaining vestiges of legal discrimination. The forecast decline in the numbers of young people entering the workforce in the 1990s has also strengthened the employment prospects of women, particularly married women.

Appendix III:
Women at Work and in Public
Life: Some Important 'Firsts'

1919 Woman Member of Parliament to take a seat in the House of Commons, Nancy Astor.

1929 Cabinet minister, Margaret Bondfield.

1943 President of the Trades Union Congress, Anne Loughlin.

1945 Prison governor, Charity Taylor.

1948 University vice-chancellor, Professor Lillian Penson.

1949 King's Counsel (Senior Barrister), Rose Heilbron and Helena Normanton.

1955 Head of Civil Service Department (Permanent Secretary), Evelyn Sharp.

1958 Life Peeress, Baroness Wootton of Abinger.
Bank manager, Hilda Harding.

1964 British Nobel Prizewinner (for chemistry), Dorothy Hodgkin.

1965 High Court judge, Elizabeth Lane.

1973 British High Commissioner, Eleanor Emery. Director of a national museum (the Science Museum), Margaret Weston.

1974 Captain of the Gentlemen-at-Arms (Government Chief Whip, House of Lords), Lady Llewelyn Davies.

1975 Leader of the official Opposition, Margaret Thatcher.

1976 British Ambassador, Anne Warburton.

1979 Prime Minister, Margaret Thatcher.
President of the British Medical Association, Josephine Barnes.

1981 Leader of the House of Lords, Baroness Young.

1983 Lord Mayor of London, Dame Mary Donaldson.

1984 Law Commissioner, Brenda Hoggett. Trade union general secretary (Society of Graphical and Allied Trades [SOGAT] '82), Brenda Dean.

1987 Court of Appeal judge, Dame Elizabeth Butler-Sloss.

1990 Royal Navy chaplain, Reverend Caroline Pullman.

Appendix IV:
Important Advances for Women's Rights

1869 Women ratepayers get the vote in local elections.

1907 Women win right to be elected as county or borough councillors.

1918 Women over 30 get the right to vote in general elections: Representation of the People Act.
Women win right to be elected as members of the House of Commons: Parliament (Qualification of Women) Act.

1919 Right of entry to most professions formally granted to women: Sex Discrimination (Removal) Act.

1928 All women over 21 get the vote: Representation of the People (Equal Franchise) Act.

1945 Family allowances paid direct to mothers: Family Allowances Act.

1969 Wives can enter into financial and legal contracts in their own right: Family Law Reform Act.

1970 Right to equal treatment where men and women do the same or broadly similar work: Equal Pay Act.

1973 Equal rights of guardianship of children for both parents: Guardianship Act.

1975 Sex discrimination unlawful in employment, training, education, and the provision of housing, services, goods and facilities to the public: Sex Discrimination Act.
Right to paid maternity leave and other rights for working women: Employment Protection Act.

1980 Equality of entitlement to most social security benefits: Social Security Act.

1983 Equal pay for women for work of equal value: Equal Pay (Amendment) Regulations.

1986 Equal retirement ages for men and women: Sex Discrimination Act.

1988 Independent taxation for husband and wife: Finance Act.

Addresses

Department of Education and Science, Elizabeth House, York Road, London SE1 7PH.

Department of Employment, Caxton House, Tothill Street, London SW1H 9NF.

Department of Health, Richmond House, 79 Whitehall, London SW1A 2NS.

Department of Social Security, Richmond House, 79 Whitehall, London SW1A 2NS.

Equal Opportunities Commission, Overseas House, Quay Street, Manchester M3 3HN.

Equal Opportunities Commission for Northern Ireland, Chamber of Commerce House, Great Victoria Street, Belfast BT2 2BA.

Home Office, Queen Anne's Gate, London SW1H 9AT.

Commission of the European Communities, 8 Storey's Gate, London SW1P 3AT.

Women's National Commission, Government Offices, Horse Guards Road, London SW1P 3AL.

Further Reading

£

Equal Opportunities Commission.
Annual Report.   HMSO

Equal Opportunities Commission for
Northern Ireland.
Annual Report.   EOC for Northern Ireland

Career Break and Childcare Provisions in
the Civil Service: A Review of Progress 1989.
Office of the Minister for the Civil Service.
ISBN 0 7115 0166 1.   Cabinet Office   1989

Lone-Parent Families—Combining Family
Responsibilities with Paid Employment.
Women's National Commission.   Cabinet Office   1989

Public Appointments: A Handbook for
Women's Organisations.
Women's National Commission.   Cabinet Office   1990

Violence Against Women: Report of an
Ad Hoc Working Group.
Women's National Commission.   Cabinet Office   1985

Women's Organisations in the United
Kingdom 1989–90.
Women's National Commission.   Cabinet Office   1990

Equal Pay for Men and Women:
Strengthening the Acts: Formal
Proposals. Equal Opportunities Commission.
ISBN 1 870358 08 2.   EOC   1990

£

*From Policy to Practice: An Equal
Opportunities Strategy for the 1990s.*
Equal Opportunities Commission.   EOC   1989

Some Facts About Women 1990. Equal
Opportunities Commission.   EOC   1990

*Towards Equality: A Casebook of Decisions
on Sex Discrimination and Equal Pay
1976–1986.* Equal Opportunities
Commission.   EOC   1989   10·00

*Women and Public Appointments: Guidelines
for Government Departments.* Equal
Opportunities Commission and Public
Appointments Unit.   EOC   1988

*Equal Opportunities for Women in the Civil
Service: Progress Report 1990.* Office of the
Minister for the Civil Service.
ISBN 0 11 430049 6.   HMSO   1990   2·50

*Report of the Committee of Inquiry into
Human Fertilisation and Embryology.*
Cmnd 9314. Department of Health and Social
Security. ISBN 0 10 193140 9.   HMSO   1984   6·40

*Women and Men in Britain 1990. Comparative
Gender-Related Statistics for England,
Scotland and Wales—Including Sub-Regional
Breakdowns.* Equal Opportunities Commission.
ISBN 0 11 701497 4.   HMSO   1990   6·20

*The Nairobi Forward-Looking Strategies for the
Advancement of Women: A Review.*   Home Office   1987

£

Sex Discrimination. A Guide to the
Sex Discrimination Act 1975.   Home Office   1978

Women, Development and the British Aid
Programme: A Progress Report. Overseas
Development Administration.   ODA   1989

Sex Discrimination: A Guide to the Sex
Discrimination (Northern Ireland) Orders
1976 and 1988.
Department of Economic Development,
                          Northern Ireland   1988

The Report of the Hansard Society Commission
on Women at the Top.
ISBN 0 900432 21 7.   Hansard Society   1990   7·50

'Women at the top: the case of British
national policies' (Susan McRae),
Parliamentary Affairs.
July 1990.   Oxford University Press   1990

Women in the Professions: A Report
by the United Kingdom Inter-professional Group.
ISBN 1 85328 062 3.   Law Society   1990   4·95

Women and Men in Britain 1991.
Equal Opportunities Commission.   HMSO   1991   9·95

The Key to Real Choice: An Action
Plan for Childcare. Equal Opportunities
Commission.   EOC   1990   5·00

Many other publications on equal opportunities are published
by the Equal Opportunities Commissions, the Department of
Employment, the Women's National Commission, and the
Commission of the European Communities; publications lists
may be obtained from these organisations at the addresses on
p. 90.

Written by Reference Services,
Central Office of Information.

Printed in the UK for HMSO.
Dd 295009 c40 12/91